ADELPHON KRUPTOS

$\mathscr{A}$DELPHON $\mathscr{K}$RUPTOS

THE SECRET RITUAL OF THE KNIGHTS OF LABOR

Reprinted from the 1886 Ezra Cook edition,
edited and with an introduction by

SAMUEL WAGAR

Westphalia Press
An Imprint of the Policy Studies Organization
Washington, DC
2016

ADELPHON KRUPTOS
All Rights Reserved 2016
by Westphalia Press
Copyright ©2016

ISBN-10: 1-63391-322-8
ISBN-13: 978-1-63391-322-6

PRINTED IN THE UNITED STATES OF AMERICA

Daniel Gutierrez-Sandoval, Executive Director
PSO and Westphalia Press

Book cover and interior design
by Jeffrey Barnes
jbarnesbook.design

Westphalia Press
An imprint of Policy Studies Organization
1527 New Hampshire Ave., NW
Washington, DC. 20036
info@ipsonet.org

Contents

Although I have rearranged the order of the material and made some small grammatical changes, this publication contains all of the text and illustrations of the Ezra Cook edition of 1886. The only additional material is the cover illustration, my introduction, and the suggestions for further research. ~ S.W.

An Introduction

By Samuel Wagar

The *Adelphon Kruptos* is the secret ritual manual of a working-class fraternal order, The Noble and Holy Order of the Knights of Labor, which grew from its beginning in 1869 in Philadelphia to become a mass movement of roughly a million members at its height in 1887. It combined the world of the fraternal secret orders that were a prominent feature of the social landscape in the English-speaking world in the late nineteenth century, with the socialist movement that was growing rapidly during the same period. The socialism of the Knights was not, however, the Marxist socialism that came to dominate the left in the period after the great depression of the 1890s, but an ethical and co-operative socialist vision with more in common with Edward Bellamy's Nationalist ideas or Theosophical ethical socialism.

The Knights were the first great trade union movement in the United States and Canada. Many leaders of the later waves of unionism received their training and inspiration from their vision of a co-operative commonwealth – ranging from Samuel Gompers, initiated into the Order in 1873 and founder of the American Federation of Labor, to the radicals of the Industrial Workers of the World and the Congress of Industrial Organization.

The Knights were a cultural movement as much as a movement of the proletariat, with goals broader than reforming the relations of production. They saw themselves as reworking society on behalf of the working class, and they included both skilled and unskilled, black, white and brown workers (although, to their lasting shame, not Asian origin workers), and women and men. They established co-operative enterprises and advocated for arbitration over conflict and a surprising number of their policies, such as equal pay for women and men, still have not been realized.

Due to a variety of factors – the extremely rapid growth of the organization and a very large degree of local autonomy leading to weak leadership, the strong reaction from the capitalist class and the state to the wave of strikes and riots in the late 1880s, faction fighting inside the organization between socialists, anarchists, and business unionists and the ambivalence of the Knights' leadership to class struggle, including the use of strikes or the autonomous organization of working class political parties, the Knights of Labor collapsed in the 1890s and early 1900s. However, its legacy is rich and it continues to influence trade union organization and working class culture to the present, more than a hundred years later.

What is particularly significant about the *Adelphon Kruptos*, which makes the document so interesting to me, is its sense of the moral power and nobility of labour, the clear portrait of personal worth being measured and validated through productive labour. It is an emotionally resonant restatement of Marx's cool and intellectual analysis of estranged labour and a determination, through fraternalism, to reclaim labour as "noble and holy" and to reclaim the products of labour for moral reasons. It points toward a cultural and ethical socialist vision, whose time may have come again, after the collapse of the Leninist regimes and the lacklustre adjustments of social democracy.

A note on the source is in order here – although the publishing house, Ezra A. Cook, opposed secret societies and published a number of sets of their rituals in order to discredit them, their exposés were accurate. Mark C. Carnes, in **Secret Ritual and**

Manhood in Victorian America (1989) documents the exposés and the ciphers and keys later published to argue for the accuracy of Cook's publications. His examination of the Knights of Labor material is on page 163. A partial French language *Adelphon Kruptos* from the Quebec Knights is also available on microfilm (CIHM 47750) and it corresponds to portions of Cook's *A.K.*

I've added a list of suggested texts for those who are interested in following up on the *A.K.* and learning more about the Knights of Labor at the end of this book.

Samuel Wagar is a Doctor of Ministry student at St. Stephen's College in Edmonton, the Wiccan chaplain at University of Alberta, and he retains a passionate interest in ritual and the creation of ethical community. swagar@ualberta.ca

OPENING SERVICES

DIAGRAM OF KNIGHTS OF LABOR LODGE ROOM.

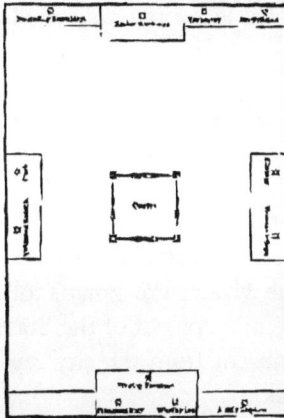

A Globe being placed on the outside of the Outer Veil; a box or basket, containing blank cards on a Triangular Table, red in colour, in the centre of the vestibule; a Lance on the outside of the Inner Veil, or entrance to the Hall, over the wicket; that the initiated may know that an Assembly of the Knights of Labor is in session.

The Master Workman will proceed to open the Assembly in due form, as follows:

Precisely at the hour for opening, allowing five minutes for difference in time pieces, the Master Workman, standing at the Capital shall give one rap and say; *"All persons not entitled to sit with us will please retire."* The Worthy Inspector then takes the Globe and Lance and proceeds to mark the Outer and Inner Veils with them.

Previous to that all persons were at liberty to enter the room, but the Veils are then closed and none can enter without giving the Password. When the Worthy Inspector goes to the Outer Veil to put the Globe in its place, the Outside Esquire takes position in the anteroom, and when the Worthy Inspector enters the Inner Veil, the Inside Esquire takes position at Inner Veil.

When the Worthy Inspector returns, the Master Workman will say:

Master Workman: *The proper officer will see that all present are entitled to sit with us, and make the proper record in the Master Workman's roll-book.*

The Worthy Inspector examines all present, and makes the proper record in the Master Workman's roll-book. Members at a distance of three miles, or out of the State; any one reported sick, or members absent from the city reporting by letter, receive a present mark.

When done the Worthy Inspector reports as follows:

Worthy Inspector: *Master Workman, I have examined all and find them entitled to sit with us.*

Master Workman: *Worthy Foreman, see that the Veils are properly marked and securely closed. Allow none to enter or retire during the opening of the Assembly.*

The Worthy Foreman brings the Outside Esquire in, after attending carefully to the duties, and reports thus:

Worthy Foreman: *Master Workman, the Veils are properly marked and securely closed.*

The Master Workman will give three raps. Officers and members will form a circle around the centre, Officers in front of their station as near as possible. Turning to the Venerable Sage, the Master Workman will say:

Master Workman: *Venerable Sage, what are the duties of the Master Workman?*

Venerable Sage: *To preside with impartiality; see that all mandates are faithfully executed. In case of emergency, where no law exists, the best judgement of the Master Workman should be used for the interest and welfare of all members, submitting the action taken for the approval or disapproval of the Assembly, and be ready at all times, in season and out of season, to advance the interest and welfare of each member.*

Master Workman: *All of which duties I will, to the best of my ability, do and perform, according to my pledge of honour. And now, Venerable sage, what are the duties of a true Knight?*

Venerable Sage: *The duties of a true Knight are to render all possible assistance to a member; to be ever watchful for opportunities whereby a member may be benefited; to report to the Master Workman all matters of advantage for the Executive Head of the Assembly to know, and at all times give strict obedience to the Master Workman.*

Master Workman: *All eyes on the Master Workman and simultaneously follow my motions.*

1st POSITION.   2nd POSITION.

The Master Workman then gives the Sign of Obliteration: (Place the palm of the right hand on the palm of the left hand – both hands in front of the body at the height of the elbow – elbows close to the body – right hand uppermost. Then separate the hands, right and left as if wiping something off the left hand with the right – elbows still touching the sides – right palm down – left palm up. Then drop both hands naturally to sides.

(**Special Instructions to Master Workman** – Do not bring the hands together with a slap or noise – an error in some locals. Do not hold the hands higher than the elbows. In separating the hands do not throw them out sidewise beyond a line with the body. This sign being used more than any other, strive to have your members make it in an easy and graceful manner.)

Master Workman: *Officers and members will now take their stations and remain standing until the charter is displayed.*

When all are at their stations, the Master Workman will issue the Order of Opening, as follows:

Master Workman: *And now, by the power in me vested, I declare this Assembly duly and regularly opened for the transaction of such business as may be lawfully brought before it; giving due notice and caution to each member to observe that dignity and decorum that should characterize true Knights, for should angry discussion or disorderly conduct arise, I shall at once avail myself of the laws of Knighthood, and immediately close theAssembly.*

When done, give one rap, and all will be seated, and the Order of Business will be commenced.

ALTERNATIVE OPENING

Should the Master Workman determine, on account of want of time, to omit the formal Opening, and no objection being made, shall, at the Opening say:

Master Workman: *We will open the Assembly by Proclamation.* (Three raps).

All form in a circle around the centre.

Master Workman: *All eyes on the Master Workman and follow my motions.* All led by Master Workman make the Sign of Obliteration.

Master Workman: *And now, by the power in me vested, I declare this Assembly opened by Proclamation for the transaction of such business as may be lawfully brought before it; giving due notice and caution to each member to observe that dignity and decorum that should characterize true Knights, for should angry discussion or disorderly conduct arise, I shall at once avail myself of the laws of Knighthood, and immediately close the Assembly.*

ORDER OF BUSINESS

1. Roll Call of Officers.

2. Reading the Minutes of last Assembly, and action thereon.

3. Clear the Secretary's table of all documents, correspondence, etc.

4. Consider previous proposals and balloting for

candidates (see "Law of the Ballot" at the end of this section.)

5. Initiation

6. Finance. Collect dues, draw orders for bills read. Clear the tables of the Financial Secretary and Treasurer of all financial business.

7. Labour: Ask the two principal questions of the Session, viz: *First*: Are there any vacancies known in the trade to be filled? *Second*: Are any of our members out of employment, seeking engagements or wishing to change? Discuss Labour in all its interests. Clear the Master Workman's table. Report and collect Statistics. Clear the Statistician's table.

8. Propositions for membership. (At each proposition say: *It is now lawful and necessary to give any facts in your possession as to the propriety or impropriety of conferring the honour.*)

9. Report of the Almoner.

10. Reports of Standing and Special Committees.

11. Unfinished Business.

12. New Business. Bureau Business of all kinds: Statistics, Mechanics, Science, Essays, Poems, Reading, etc. Election of Officers according to the laws of Knighthood, and Installation, are in order any time after opening. In cases of emergency, the members must be notified by Lawful Summons, accompanied by the Great seal of Knighthood, when each one will be required imperatively to

be in place, and the Worthy Inspector shall record each one present in red colour. This is called a Red Letter Day or Assembly, and absence at that time works dishonour to an absentee, and incurs such penalty as the Assembly by its By-Laws may impose as a violation of the third paragraph of the pledge.

LAW OF THE BALLOT

The Ballot-box must be placed at the Centre, which shall be announced by the Master Workman, also the names and occupation of the candidate or candidates to be balloted for.

Knights must make the Sign of Obliteration before depositing the ballot. In every Assembly of three hundred members or less, three black balls are required to reject, and an additional black ball for every additional hundred members or majority fraction thereof. Should there be one or two black balls in the ballot box, it shall be so announced by Worthy Foreman and Master Workman, which will postpone the consideration of the candidate until next stated meeting of the Assembly and it shall be the duty of the Knight or Knights depositing the black balls to give their objections in writing to the Master Workman before the next stated Assembly which objections shall be read by the Master Workman at the next stated Assembly. The signature of the opposing Knight shall not be read or made known by the Master Workman. After the objections are read by the Master Workman, so that all may fully understand the objections made, the Master Workman shall, in the presence of all Knights, burn the paper, so that the writing is all destroyed, and order another ballot, when the question shall be asked by the Master Workman: *Are the objections sufficient to reject the candidate from the honour of Knighthood?* If, at the previous ballot, but one black ball was announced, and at the second ballot two appear, the candidate shall be declared rejected. If, at the previous ballot, two black balls were announced, and at the second ballot one appear, the candidate shall be declared rejected.

The Master Workman must see that the Knight or Knights who have delivered their objections do not vote to sustain their objections at the second ballot. Should the Knight or Knights who voted black balls fail to make known their objections on or before the next stated Assembly, the Master Workman shall make the statement in open Assembly that such is the case, and also that the candidate is duly elected, the objections not being sustained.

When a candidate is rejected by the Law of this ballot, it shall be unlawful for the candidate to be again proposed or balloted for in any Assembly of the Knights of Labor for the space of six months, dating from said rejection.

It is optional for any Assembly to receive propositions of membership from any persons under the age of eighteen and over sixteen years.

INITIATION

The Master Workman will direct the Unknown Knight to go to the Vestibule and obtain the names and occupations of the candidates in waiting, return to the Assembly, and report to the Master Workman. If the candidates reported are endorsed by the Recording Secretary as having been duly proposed, balloted for and elected, the Unknown Knight will return to the Vestibule and make the prescribed examination. If the examination is satisfactory the Unknown Knight will announce them to the Inside Esquire who will announce them to the Master Workman who will direct them to be admitted. The Unknown

Knight will proceed to the opening in the circle, and introduce them to the Master Workman, who will order the candidates to be placed at the centre and the pledge administered, and the Initiation proceeded with as per usage.

Master Workman: *Does anyone know cause why the candidate should not be covered by our shield and admitted into this Order?*

When any one may lawfully object by giving good reasons. The assembly shall then consider the same, and a majority vote shall decide. If no objections are made or sustained, the Master Workman shall proceed:

Master Workman: *Unknown Knight, you will proceed to the Vestibule and make the prescribed examination; if the candidate accepts, proceed to the opening and introduce the candidate.*

The Unknown Knight retires and proceeds as follows:

Unknown Knight: *Are you now or have you ever been a member of the Order of the Knights of Labor?*

Candidate: *No*

Unknown Knight: *Are you willing to bind yourself with a pledge of honour to Secrecy, Obedience, and Mutual Assistance, that will not interfere with any religious convictions you may entertain, or with your duty to your country?*

Candidate: *I am.*

The Master Workman has, previously to their entering, formed the Assembly in a circle around the centre, leaving an opening in front of the Worthy Foreman's station, hands joined, arms crossed, right arm over left, palm down, left arm under right, palm up. The Unknown Knight halts at the opening and says:

Unknown Knight: *Master Workman, our friend has satisfactorily answered all inquiries, and now desires to be covered with our shield, and admitted to fellowship in this Order.*

(When more than one candidate is Initiated, the language should be changed to the plural number when necessary.)

After a short pause, and in perfect silence, the Master Workman will say:

Master Workman: *Place our friend at the centre, and administer the pledge of honour.*

The Unknown Knight places the candidate at the centre with directions to place the left hand on the heart and raise the right hand.

The Unknown Knight then administers the following pledge, which the candidate must repeat:

Obligation: *I do truly promise, on my honour, that I will never reveal to any person or persons whatsoever, any of the signs, or secret workings of the Order that may be now or hereafter confided to me, any acts done or objects intended, except in a lawful and authorized manner, or by special permission of the Order granted to me.*

That I will not reveal to any employer or other person the name or person of anyone a member of the Order without permission of the member.

That I will strictly obey all laws and lawful summons that may be sent, said, or handed to me, and that, during my connection with the Order, I will, to the best of my ability, defend the life, interest, reputation and family of all true members of this Order: help and assist all employed and unemployed, unfortunate or distressed members to procure employ, and secure just remuneration; relieve their distress, and counsel others to aid them, so that they and theirs may receive and enjoy the just fruits of their labor and exercise of their art. And I do further promise that I will, without reservation or evasion, consider the pledge of secrecy I have taken binding upon me until death.

The Master Workman gives one tap to seat the Assembly. The Unknown Knight will, after the Assembly is seated, proceed with the candidate to the capitol, and report to the Master Workman.

Unknown Knight: *Master Workman, our friend has taken the pledge of secrecy, obedience, and mutual assistance.*

Master Workman: *That act covers our friend with the shield of our Order. Proceed with the candidate to the Base, there to receive the instructions of the Worthy Foreman.*

Arrived at the Base, the Unknown Knight introduces the candidate to the Worthy Foreman, thus:

Unknown Knight: *Worthy Foreman, by permission of this Assembly of true Knights and the command of the Master Workman, I present our friend for instruction.*

Worthy Foreman: *By labour is brought forth the kindly fruits of the Earth in rich abundance for our sustenance and comfort; by labour, (not exhaustive), are promoted health of body and strength of mind; and labour garners the priceless stores of wisdom and knowledge. It is the "Philosopher's Stone" – everything it touches turns to wealth. "Labour is noble and holy." To defend it from degradation, to divest it of the evils of body, mind, and estate, which ignorance and greed have imposed; to rescue the toiler from the grasp of the selfish is a work worthy of the noblest and best of our race. You have been selected from among your associates for that exalted purpose. Are you willing to accept the responsibility, and, trusting in the support of pledged true Knights, labor, with what ability you possess, for the triumph of these principles among men?*

The candidate answers. If affirmatively, the Worthy Foreman will say to the candidate and the Unknown Knight:

Worthy Foreman: *We will now proceed with our friend to the Master Workman.*

And, accompanying them to the Master Workman, says:

Worthy Foreman: *Master Workman, I present our friend as a fitting and worthy person to receive the honour of fellowship with this noble Order.*

The Master Workman, taking his hand, will say:

Master Workman: *On behalf of the toiling millions of Earth, I welcome you to this Order, pledged to the service of Humanity.*

Open and public associations having failed, after a struggle of centuries, to protect or advance the interest of labour, we have lawfully constituted this assembly. Hid from public view, we are covered by a veil of secrecy, not to promote or shield wrong-doing, but to shield ourselves and you from persecution and wrong by men in our own sphere and calling, as well as others out of it, when we endeavour to secure the just reward of our toil. In using this power of organized effort and cooperation, we but imitate the example of capital heretofore set in numberless instances. In all the multifarious branches of trade, capital has its combinations; and whether intended or no, they crush the manly hopes of labour and trample poor humanity in the dust.

We mean no conflict with legitimate enterprise, no antagonism to necessary capital; but men, in their haste and greed, blinded by self-interests, overlook the interests of others, and sometimes violate the rights of those they deem helpless.

We mean to uphold the dignity of labor; to affirm the nobility of all who earn their bread by the sweat of their brow. We mean to create a healthy public opinion on the subject of labour (the only creator of values and capital) and the justice of it receiving a full, just share of the values or capital it has created. We shall, with all our strength, support laws made to harmonize the interests of labour and capital, for labour alone gives life and value to capital, and also those laws, which tend to lighten the exhaustiveness of toil.

We shall use every lawful and honourable means to procure and retain employ for one another, coupled with just and fair remuneration; and should accident or misfortune befall any of our number, render such aid as lies within our power to give, without inquiring their country or creed, and without approving of general strikes among artisans; yet should it become justly necessary to enjoin an oppressor, we will protect and aid any of our members who thereby may suffer loss, and as opportunity offers, extend a helping hand to all branches of honourable toil.

Such is but an epitome of our objects. Your duties and obligations, your privileges and benefits, you will learn as you mingle with and become acquainted with the noble Order of the Knights of Labor.

Master Workman: *Unknown Knight, conduct the candidate to the Venerable sage at the centre for instructions in the work of an Assembly.*

The Unknown Knight now conducts the candidate to the Venerable Sage who instructs in the signs and their language, the symbols and their significance, and the rules and usages of an Assembly, as follows:

Venerable Sage: *The entrances to this Assembly are known as Veils. We style the room to which you were first admitted the Vestibule. The one in which you now stand is known as the Sanctuary.*

The symbol of the Outer Veil is a Globe, symbolizing the field of our operation, and signifies "Universal Organization." It is always placed on the outside as a sure indication that an Assembly is inside and in session. To gain admission, give any alarm and the pass-word. [Which for the last half of 1886 is "Discourage Discord."] The word "Discourage" is given at the outer door and "Discord" at the inner door and both are given together to Worthy Inspector when he takes up the pass-word at opening of Assembly, in a whisper to the Outside Esquire. When in the Vestibule, write your full name, official standing and the number of your Assembly on a card.

The symbol of the Inner Veil is a Lance, and signifies "Defence," placed on the outside. To gain admission, give the entering signal.

ENTERING SIGNAL – INNER VEIL

Three raps; given in this peculiar manner: One; a short pause – then two in quick succession.

When the Inside Esquire attends, pass in your card. The Inside Es-quire will deliver it to the Worthy Foreman who will announce it to the Assembly in a distinct tone of voice, so that all may know who is in waiting. If you are entitled to admission, the Worthy Foreman will direct the Inside Esquire to call you by name, when you will advance and give the explanation of pass-word, ["discord" for the last half of 1886,] in a whisper to the Inside Esquire when you will be admitted.

The Venerable sage as Librarian of the Assembly is stationed in the centre on the left. The symbol of the centre is a Book, and signifies "Knowledge." When admitted to the Assembly, immediately ad-vance to the centre and deliver the Sign of Obliteration to the Ven-erable sage, who sits there to represent the dignity of the Order. It is made thus:

SIGN OF OBLITERATION

1st POSITION. 2nd POSITION.

Place the palm of the right hand on the palm of the left hand – both hands in front of the body at the height of the elbow – elbows close to the body – right hand uppermost.

Then separate the hands, right and left as if wiping something off the left hand with the right –elbows still touching the sides – right palm down – left palm up. Then drop both hands naturally to sides.

The language of that sign is: "to erase, obliterate, wipe out" everything on entering here, as the draughtsman erases useless lines.

On retiring, you also come to the center and deliver the same sign, when it also signifies to obliterate, or to keep profoundly secret, everything seen, heard, said, or done by yourself or others, absolutely in accordance with your pledge. It is answered by the Venerable sage by the Sign of Decoration thus:

SIGN OF DECORATION

Place the index finger of the right hand on the left breast, back of the hand to the front. The language of the answering sign is:

"Labor is noble and holy."

The grip is made thus:

GRIP

Extend the hand with the thumb parallel with the forefinger and close to it; clasp hands with the fingers, without locking the thumbs – with a side pressure of the thumbs on the outside – thumbs still extended parallel with each other. Then end locking the thumbs and an ordinary shake of the hands.

The grip signifies "Humanity". As the thumb distinguishes man from all other orders of creation, and by it alone man is able to achieve wonders of art and perform labor, we always, therefore, approach a member in this way, after which shake hands in the usual way.

1st POSITION.

2nd POSITION.

SIGN OF INTELLIGENCE

The Sign of Intelligence is made by placing the index finger of the right hand in the centre of the forehead – the last three fingers of the hand closed over the thumb – back of the hand to the front.

The language of that sign is: "I have determined," that being the seat of intelligence and wisdom. It is used in voting both in the affirmative and negative.

SIGN OF RECOGNITION

The sign is made with shield or left hand, thus: with the thumb and first two fingers of the left hand take hold of the end of the right sleeve, at the cuff on the right hand – thumb on the outside and the two fingers inserted on the inside. Make a motion as if to turn up the cuff.

The language of that sign is: "I am a worker," to be used in strange company or among or where craftsmen are employed, to ascertain if there are Knights present.

ANSWER

The answer is made in this manner: Draw the right hand open across the forehead from left to right, back of hand to the front.

The language of the answer is: "I, too, earn my bread by the sweat of my brow." To give assurance, if necessary, use it in reverse, the challenged giving the sign, and challenger giving the answer.

We also have a verbal challenge:

VERBAL CHALLENGE

The following words are used where a member might be seeking for work or information: "I have come," a member replying to the challenge with; "work your way." Any other words can be used after the words "come" and "way" so as not to attract attention, such as "I have come to look for work," and "work your way and find it."

THE CRY OF DISTRESS

To be used in the dark, or when the Sign of Recognition cannot be used, is thus: "I am a stranger," giving emphasis to the word stranger. *Any member of the Order hearing this will answer; "a stranger should be assisted."*

CAUTION

As the value of the cry of distress, for practical use, depends entirely on accuracy of wording, great care should be exercised in instructing candidates, especially as great irregularity now exists. The words given above are all of the official work, although members are allowed to supplement the words given with others, so as not to attract attention from those not members, as for instance: "I am a stranger and need assistance." Answer: "a stranger should be assisted and I for one am willing to help you." Any other similar additional words may be used, but when instructing candidates use care not to confound the official part with the unofficial.

The sign of caution is made in this manner:

SIGN OF CAUTION

Close the last two fingers of the right hand, leaving the first fingers extended. Place the two extended fingers on the left side of the forehead – back of hand to the front. Then draw the fingers across the forehead toward the right and down over the right side of the face, then cross the mouth toward the left, the thumb under the line, in a careless manner.

It is used to warn any member whom you may see being imposed upon or cheated; or where a member is thoughtlessly revealing in the presence of those not members something in regard to the Order that should only be known to members.

In balloting, advance to the centre; deliver the Sign of Obliteration to the Master Workman, who will answer by the Sign of Decoration. You will then deposit your ballot and retire.

The special meeting sign is a perpendicular and horizontal line, meeting at right angles. The hour of meeting is placed over the horizontal *line; the number of the Local under it. The month, designated by a figure, as 3 for March, is placed to the left of the* perpendicular *line; the day of the month to the right of it. The horizontal line may be placed either at the top or bottom of the perpendicular line, and may run either to the right or left of it. The horizontal line may be placed either at the top or bottom of the perpendicular line, and may run either to the right or left of it. All that is required is two lines, one horizontal and the other perpendicular, meeting at right angles. When the hour of meeting is* before *noon, the sign X is placed* before *the hour of meeting. When it is* after *noon, then* after *the hour.*

Wishing to announce a special meeting of Local Assembly No. 300 for September 5th, at 8 o'clock in the evening it is done as shown by figure.

This Assembly is known as _____ *Assembly No.* _____ *, and is attached to (*the General Assembly, or District Assembly, No _____, as the case may be.*) Your monthly dues are* _____ *cents, and upon your prompt payment of the same to the Financial Secretary will depend, in a great measure, your good standing in the Order.*

Unknown Knight, you will please conduct the candidate to the Master Workman for the closing ceremony.

The instructions of the Venerable Sage may extend to the various officers, bureaus, emblems, etc., as the Master Workman may direct, or it may be resumed later in the session, and while other business is being transacted, by a competent member. If closed here, the candidate is conducted to the Master Workman for the following address, which is given extempore, and must contain the following points:

Master Workman: *The only jewels worn by the Order are those of the heart – honour and fraternity. The only regalia is that of neat, tidy dress. The only conduct, cordial, harmonious and fraternal. Observe these at all times and you will confer a great favour upon this Order.*

The candidate may now be presented to the Financial Secretary, Worthy Inspector, etc., and instructed in the duties of their offices, while the business of the assembly is being proceeded with in regular order.

RECESS

In going into recess, the Master Workman will give three raps, calling the members of the Assembly in a circle, when, with all eyes upon the Master Workman, all will give the sign of Obliteration. After which the Master Workman will say:

Master Workman; *I now declare this Assembly at recess for the space of _____ minutes, for the purpose of congratulating and welcoming our new member.*

At the conclusion of the recess, the Master Workman gives two raps. The members assemble in circle, all eyes on the Master Workman, and deliver the Sign of Obliteration.

The Master Workman gives one rap to seat the members, and says:

Master Workman: *I now declare this Assembly in regular session.*

CLOSING

Master Workman: *If all are satisfied and ready, we will proceed to close. The Worthy Inspector will see that the charter and secret work are securely bestowed.*

While the Worthy Inspector and Assistants are safely securing the Books and other property of the Assembly, the Master Workman may, in a few well-chosen words, thank the members for their presence, the dignity, courtesy and fraternal conduct observed during Assembly; commend and enforce the harmony and union that has prevailed and should ever prevail in the Assembly; and in short, pithy phrase, draw attention to any business pressing for attention in the future.

Give three raps, form circle around the centre.

Master Workman: *All eyes on the Master Workman and follow my motions.*

All deliver the Sign of Obliteration, after which the Master Workman says:

Master Workman: *And now, by the power in me vested, I declare this Assembly duly and regularly closed until _____ at _____ o'clock, but should matters of importance require a special session, each one shall have due notice thereof.*

One rap.

FOUNDING CEREMONY

Newly-organized Local Assemblies only are required to be Founded. When a Local Assembly lapses and is reorganized, the Founding Ceremony is not again performed. The Founding

Ceremony can only be performed by a regularly commissioned Organizer or any General Officer holding a certificate of election from the General Assembly.

Upon organizing a new Local Assembly, the Organizer will arrange the time and place of meeting, and promptly at the appointed time will take the station at the Capital and call the assemblage to order: after which display the Commission as Organizer in front of the Capital and announce as follows:

Organizer: *By authority of the General Assembly of America, of the Order of the Knights of Labor, delegated to me by this Commission, I appear at this time for the purpose of Founding and instituting a Local Assembly of the Order.*

The alarming development and aggressiveness of great capitalists and corporations, unless checked, will inevitably lead to the pauperization and hopeless degradation of the toiling masses. It is imperative, if we desire to enjoy the full blessings of life, that a check be placed upon unjust accumulation, and the power for evil of aggregated wealth.

This much-desired object can be accomplished only by the united efforts of those who obey the Divine injunction, "In the sweat of thy face shalt thou eat bread." Therefore, you have been invited to join us in an organization that embraces within its folds every department of productive industry, whose aims are;

- *To make industrial and moral worth, not wealth, the true standard of individual and National greatness.*

- *To secure to the workers the full enjoyment of the wealth they create, sufficient leisure in which to develop their intellectual, moral and social faculties; all of the benefits, recreation and pleasures of association; in a word, to enable them to share in the gains and honours of advancing civilization.*

KRUPTOS.

In order to secure these results, you will be expected to work with and aid us in demanding at the hands of the State the following objects, which are equally binding upon you and your successors while the Assembly lasts:

- *The establishment of Bureaus of Labour Statistics that we may arrive at a correct knowledge of the educational, moral and financial condition of the laboring masses.*

- *That the public lands, the heritage of the people, be reserved for actual settlers; not another acre for railroads or speculators; and that all lands now held for speculative purposes be taxed to their full value.*

- *The abrogation of all laws that do not bear equally upon capital and labour, and the removal of unjust technicalities, delays and discriminations in the administration of justice.*

- *The adoption of measures providing for the health and safety of those engaged in mining, manufacturing and building industries, and for indemnification to those engaged therein for injuries received through lack of necessary safeguards.*

- *The recognition by incorporation of trades' unions, orders, and such other associations as may be organized by the working masses to improve their condition and protect their rights.*

- *The enactment of laws to compel corporations to pay their employees weekly, in lawful money, for the labour of the preceding week, and giving mechanics and labourers a first lien upon the product of their labour to the extent of their full wages.*

- *The abolition of the contract system on National, State and Municipal works.*

- *The enactment of laws providing for arbitration between employers and employed, and to enforce the decisions of the arbitrators.*

- *The prohibition, by law, of the employment of children under 15 years of age in workshops, mines and factories.*

- *To prohibit the hiring out of convict labour.*

- *That a graduated income tax be levied.*

And demanding at the hands of Congress:

- *The establishment of a National monetary system, in which a circulating medium in necessary quantity shall issue directly to the people, without the intervention of banks; that all the national issue shall be full legal tender in payment of all debts, public and private; and that the government shall not guarantee or recognize any private banks, or create any banking corporations.*

- *That interest-bearing bonds, bills of credit or notes shall never be issued by the Government, but that, when need arises, the emergency shall be met by issue of legal tender non-interest-bearing money.*

- *That the importation of foreign labour under contract be prohibited.*

- *That, in connection with the post-office, the Government shall organize financial exchanges, safe deposits, and facilities for deposit of the savings of the people in small sums.*

- *That the government shall obtain possession, by purchase, under the right of eminent domain, of all telegraphs, telephones and railroads, and that hereafter no charter or license be issued to any corporations for construction or operation of any means of transporting intelligence, passengers or freight.*

And while making the foregoing demands upon the State and National Government, will endeavour to associate our own labours:

- *To establish co-operative institutions such as will tend to supersede the wage system, by the introduction of a co-operative industrial system.*

- *To secure for both sexes equal pay for equal work.*

- *To shorten the hours of labour by a general refusal to work for more than eight hours.*

- *To persuade employers to agree to arbitrate all differences which may arise between them and their employees, in order that the bonds of sympathy between them may be strengthened and that strikes may be rendered unnecessary.*

Organizer: *Do you approve of those objects and all legitimate effort for the benefit of labour and the cause of Humanity?*

Response: *We do.*

Organizer: *Are you willing to take a pledge of secrecy, obedience and mutual assistance that will not interfere with any religious convictions you may entertain or your duty to your country?*

Response: *We are.*

The Organizer will then prepare or draft the Great Seal of

knighthood, place it at the centre, and when done, resume the station, give three raps, form the members of the new Assembly around the centre, and say:

Organizer: *Thus do I imprint the Great Seal of Knighthood at the centre, and thereby dedicate this new Assembly to the service of Humanity. Let the memory of that symbol ever remind you of the duties and obligations you owe to the cause of labour.*

The Organizer will then direct each one to place the left hand on the heart, raise the right hand, and administer the following pledge, which each one will repeat:

I do truly promise, on my honor, that I will never reveal to any person or persons whatsoever, any of the signs or secret workings of the Order that may be now or hereafter confided to me, any acts done or objects intended, except in a lawful and authorized manner, or by special permission of the Order granted to me.

That I will not reveal to any employer or other person the name or person of anyone a member of the Order without permission of the member.

That I will strictly obey all laws and lawful summons that may be sent, said or handed to me, and that, during my connection with the Order, I will, to the best of my ability, defend the life, interest, reputation and family of all true members of this Order; help and assist all employed or unemployed, unfortunate or distressed members, to procure employ, and secure just remuneration; relieve their distress, and counsel others to aid them, so that they and theirs may receive and enjoy the just fruits of their labour and exercise of their art.

And I do further promise that I will, without reservation or evasion, consider the pledge of secrecy I have taken binding upon me until death.

The Organizer then gives one rap and seats the Assembly; then advances to the centre, and standing upon the Great Seal, facing the capital, says:

Now, by the authority vested in me, I declare this assemblage duly and legally organized and Founded as a Local Assembly of the Order of the Knights of Labor of America, this _____ day of _____, in the year one thousand eight hundred and _____, and of Knighthood the _____ (see Commission,) and with such number as the General Secretary-Treasurer may assign, and empowered to work in a legal and authorized manner, under (the General Assembly or District Assembly No. _____ as the case may be.)

The Organizer then returns to the Capital and instructs the Assembly in the secret Work of a Local Assembly and the Passwords; also such matters of General Information in regard to the laws and workings of the Order and the duties of Local officers, as time will permit, after which directs the Assembly to proceed to an election of officers (if not previously elected;) then proceeds to install the officers elected in accordance with the Installation Ceremony.

INSTALLATION CEREMONY

The Venerable Sage is the legal Installing Officer in all Local Assemblies.

In a Local attached to a District Assembly, when the Venerable Sage is an officer elect, or in the absence of the Venerable Sage, the ceremony can be performed by the Senior Delegate. The Venerable Sage is never installed. In a new Assembly the ceremony will be performed by the officers performing the Founding Ceremony.

The Installation Ceremony may also be performed by any regularly commissioned Organizer, or any General Officer.

The officers cannot be installed except the Assembly is in good standing, and all taxes are paid to the General Assembly or District Assembly, under whose jurisdiction it is working.

At the time appointed for installation, the Installing Officer will take position near the Capital, and say:

Installation Officer: *In accordance with the laws and regulations of the Order, I appear with you at this time for the purposes of installing the officers of this Assembly. Have all the injunctions of the Superior Body, under which you work, been faithfully obeyed; have all taxes been paid; and are you now ready to proceed with the Ceremony of Installation?*

If there is any reason why the Ceremony cannot proceed, this is the time to make it known. There being no objections, the retiring Master Workman will say:

Master Workman: *The Laws and Regulations of the Order have been faithfully complied with, and the officers of the Assembly, having been duly elected, are now ready to be installed for the ensuing term.*

Installing Officer: *You will please direct the officers of this Assembly to surrender their stations, in order that their successors may be duly installed.*

Master Workman: *The Officers will surrender their stations in obedience to the direction of the Installing Officer.*

(Note – when installing the officers of a new Assembly the ceremony begins here.)

The Installing Officer then assumes the position of the Master Workman, and names some member to act as assistant, then says:

Installing Officer: *Worthy Assistant, you will please imprint the Great Seal of Knighthood at the centre.*

The Assistant then imprints the symbol as directed, which should be on cloth or paper, large enough to stand upon, and says:

Assistant: *The Great Seal of Knighthood is at the centre.*

The Installing Officer then says:

Installing Officer: *The Recording secretary will please announce the names of the officers elect, who, as their names are given, will form a circle around the Great Seal, as near on a line with their respective stations as possible.*

The Installing Officer will roll up or secure the charter, and immediately advances to the centre, and, after the names are read, says:

Installing Officer: *Do you, each of you, accept the position to which the members of this Assembly have elected you?*

(Officers-elect, each responding.) *I do.*

Installing Officer: *Each of you will place your left hand over your heart and raise your right hand.*

Installing Officer: *You will, each of you, repeat the following pledge:*

The Installing Officer gives three raps on the Great seal of Knighthood, all members rising.

I _____ do solemnly promise, in addition to the pledge of honor already given, that I will, to the best of my ability, perform the duties of my office as laid down in the Adelphon Kruptos and Constitution, until my successor is duly elected and installed.

That I will faithfully attend the meetings of this Assembly, sacredly guard and turn over to my successor all property of the Assembly committed to my charge; and should the Assembly lapse or cease to work, I will convey and deliver all such property to the officer legally authorized to receive the same; and further, that all of my official acts while holding this position shall be just and honourable, working for the success of the Order and the triumph of its principles.

The Installing Officer gives one rap, all, except the officers, taking their respective seats.

The Installing Officer then places the gavel in the hands of the Master Workman and addresses the Master Workman, thus:

Installing Officer: *This emblem, which I now present to you, symbolizes your position and your control over this Assembly. Use it with firmness and discretion, and you cannot fail to win the support of your members. The duties of your office are defined in the Laws of the Order, in the Adelphon Kruptos, and in your obligation. Should any occasion arise, not covered by the regulations therein contained, you are expected to act according to the dictates of common sense, guided by an earnest desire for the best interests of the Order.*

The Worthy Assistant will now conduct you to your station, where, at the conclusion of the Installation Ceremony, you will take charge of your Assembly until your successor is elected and installed.

The Assistant then conducts the Master Workman to the Capital.

The Installing Officer turning to the Worthy Foreman, Worthy Inspector and Unknown Knight, addressing them thus:

Installing Officer: *You will find your duties clearly set forth in the Laws, Usages and Regulations of the Order, and when these fail to properly instruct you, it will be your duty to act, in conjunction with the Master Workman in maintaining the dignity and advancing the prosperity of the Assembly. I trust you will carefully fulfill your duties, so that you may gain not only the sanction of the members of the Assembly, but, what is of even more importance, the approval of your own conscience.*

Worthy Assistant, you will please conduct the officers to their respective stations.

The Assistant then conducts the officers to their stations.

The Installing Officer, turning to the Outside Esquire and Inside Esquire, addresses them thus:

Installing Officer: *Though your offices are apparently subordinate, do not for a moment suppose that your duties are merely nominal. To you, by the usages of the Order, is committed the admission of every person who comes within our fold.*

Guard carefully the veils, that no traitor or unworthy person may gain admittance, and by fidelity and watchfulness prove the wisdom of your selection for the trusts confided to you.

The Worthy Assistant will conduct the officers to their stations.

The Assistant then conducts them to the Veils.

The Installing Officer, turning to the Treasurer, Financial Secretary and Almoner, addresses them thus:

Installing Officer: *The duties assigned to you, covering, as they do, the financial affairs of your Assembly, particularly require accuracy and honesty. It is a proud honour to be elected for such important trusts. It is a still prouder fame to prove yourselves worthy of confidence by an official career of strict integrity and fidelity. I hope you will carefully study the duties of your respective offices, and endeavour to so act, that you can yield them to your successors with clean hands and pure hearts.*

Worthy Assistant, you will please conduct the officers to their stations.

The Assistant then conducts then to their proper stations, and the Installing Officer turns to the Recording Secretary and addresses the Recording Secretary, thus:

Installing Officer: *The duties assigned to you are of the greatest importance, as they include making a history of the acts done by your Assembly. You should strive that your records should be plainly and correctly kept, and that they should give a complete register of all transactions, not merely so that you yourself can read them, but also that any other member of the Assembly can gather from them an intelligent idea of the business acted upon. Read carefully the duties assigned to you in the Laws of the Order, and faithfully obey those provisions which set forth your duties to the higher body under which your Assembly works. Be faithful to your obligation, be just to yourself, and you cannot fail to acquit yourself so as to receive the hearty good-will of your associates.*

The Worthy Assistant will now conduct you to your station.

The Installing Officer turning to the Statistician, addresses him thus:

Installing Officer: *Your duties are important, inasmuch as, if properly performed, they will assist with the Statisticians of other Assemblies, in equalizing wages paid to labour. You should endeavour to compile a complete and accurate list of wages paid to the several trades and their subdivisions composing your Assembly, so that when called by your Assembly or the General Secretary-Treasurer you can instantly give the important information therein contained. I am confident that you will fully realize the importance of the position, and will earnestly strive faithfully to perform its duties.*

The Worthy Assistant will now escort you to your station.

The Installing Officer turning to the Judge, Judge Advocate and

Clerk, addresses them thus:

Installing Officer: *The delicate interests confided to your care will require tact and nice discrimination.*

Human nature is frail and prone to err, and, while this is so, duties such as you will perform must be provided for. Let your judgement be tempered with mercy, and even while you surely and swiftly punish wrong and treachery, do not fail to keep in mind the fact that, "To err is human, but to forgive divine."

The Worthy Assistant will now conduct you to your stations.

This having been done, the Installing Officer displays the Charter of the Assembly at the Capital. [Note – This part of the ceremony will have to be omitted in the case of a newly organized Local before the Charter has been received.]

The Installing Officer then retires to near the Inner Veil, and the Master Workman gives three raps to raise the Assembly.

The Installing Officer then hails the Assembly and says:

Installing Officer: *I hail you as Assembly No* _____, *working under a legal Charter from and issued by the authority of the General Assembly of America, and under the officers of your choice.*

In place of the above, the following form will be used at the close of the Installation Ceremony of a newly organized Local Assembly:

Installing Officer: *I hail you as a legally organized Local Assembly of the Order of the Knights of Labor of America, and entitled to work under the officers of your choice, legally installed.*

The Master Workman then directs the Assembly to give the Sign of Obliteration three times, and the Installing Officer returns the Sign of Decoration three times as Grand Honours.

The Installing Officer will then say, both hands raised:

Installing Officer: *Peace and Prosperity to the Faithful.*

Master Workman: *Worthy* (giving the Installing Officer the proper title) *you will now please approach the Capital.*

As the Installing Officer approaches the Capital, the Master Workman seats the Assembly. The Installing Officer may then address the Assembly, or the Master Workman may call upon any member or visitors from other Assemblies, if time permits.

The regular Order of Business is then resumed.

SYMBOLS AND STATIONS OF OFFICERS

MASTER WORKMAN

The Master Workman's symbol is a Column about three feet in height. The base is 10/36 of the height, in imitation of coral. The shaft 19/36 of the height, reeded in imitation of closely-bound rods. The capital 7/36 of the height, in imitation of leaves and fruit, surmounted by a human bust. The whole is an emblem of the Order, and signifies "Cooperation based based on labor creates capital when directed by intelligence." The Great Seal of Knighthood is a Triangle, surrounded by a circle.

WORTHY FOREMAN

The Worthy Foreman's symbol is a Base of Coral, and signifies "Toilers." The Worthy Foreman has control of the entrances and vestibule, the supervision of members entering and depart-ing, and, in the absence of the Master Workman, or when the Master Workman is otherwise engaged, will preside over the deliberations of the Assembly, and call a competent member to occupy the Base.

WORTHY INSPECTOR

The symbol of the Worthy Inspector is an Eye, and signifies "Watchfulness, vigilance." The Worthy Inspector examines and marks in the Master Workman's roll-book all present at the opening of the Assembly, all members admitted during the session, and all who are sick or report by letter. The roll-book governs the Master Workman as to who are best entitled to the privileges and benefits of the Assembly when more than one apply for a vacancy in employment reported to the Assembly; and present or absent marks materially affect the standing of members in the Order. The Worthy Inspector with the Financial secretary, examines all cards, and informs the Worthy Foreman whether the holders are entitled to admission. The station is in the rear of the Worthy Foreman, near the door of entrance.

ALMONER

The symbol of the Almoner is an Open Hand, and signifies "Assistance." The Almoner visits all distressed members immediately on being informed, and relieves as the case demands; notifies the Finance Committee when funds are needed, and, in cases of doubt counsels with the Master Workman; reports all transactions quarterly, concealing the names of the recipients, unless called for by a majority vote of the Assembly. The station is on the right, and by the side of the Venerable Sage.

FINANCIAL SECRETARY

The symbol of the Financial Secretary is a Coin, and signifies "Labor done." The Financial Secretary keeps a roll of members and their residences, a correct account between members and the Assembly, receives all moneys due the Assembly and pays it over to the Treasurer, taking receipt therefore. At the close of each quarter, viz: the first of January, April, July and October of each year, reports the condition of the finances and a list of arrearages of members, and, in connection with the Finance Committee, conducts the financial affairs of the Assembly. The station is in the rear of the Worthy Foreman, beside the Worthy Inspector.

WORTHY TREASURER

The symbol of the Worthy Treasurer is a Safe, and signifies "Strength." The Worthy Treasurer keeps all moneys of the Assembly, and pays out only on the order of the Assembly, attested by the Master Workman and Recording Secretary. The station is on the left of the Master Workman.

RECORDING SECRETARY

The symbol of the Recording Secretary is a Pen and Scroll, and signifies "Record." The Recording Secretary keeps a record of all transactions of the Assembly; reads all papers and documents brought before the Assembly, and performs such duties as the Assembly, by motion, directs; draws all orders on the Treasurer passed by the Assembly, attesting the same by signature and initials of office. The station is in the rear, and at the right of the Master Workman.

STATISTICIAN

The symbol of the Statistician is a Book and Flash of Lightning, and signifies "Light, knowledge and power." The Statistician shall collect from the members and all other available sources, all information attainable concerning the condition of the labouring people in the locality, and shall faithfully report the same to the District Assembly Statistician, at least once a month, and shall also report at each meeting of the Local Assembly such information as may be of service, and also to the General Secretary- Treasurer when call upon to do so. The station is to the rear, and left of the Master Workman.

UNKNOWN KNIGHT

It shall be the duty of the Unknown Knight to obtain the names and occupations of all candidates in waiting, report the same to the Master Workman, and when they are approved as having been duly proposed and elected, to make the prescribed examination and conduct candidates. The station is at the centre on the right.

VENERABLE SAGE

The symbol of the centre is a Book, and signifies "Knowledge." The Venerable sage, as Librarian of the Assembly, is stationed at the centre, on the left.

INSIDE ESQUIRE

It is the duty of the Inside Esquire to guard the Inner Veil, that no traitor or unworthy person may gain admittance; attend all signals; receive cards and deliver the same to the Worthy Foreman; receive the explanation of the Pass-word and admit no one, except by direction of the Worthy Foreman or Master Workman. Station at the Outer Veil.

OUTER ESQUIRE

It is the duty of the Outside Esquire to guard the Outer Veil; receive the password from all except candidates or visitors from another District; and preserve order in the Vestibule. Station at the Outer Veil.

LOCAL COURT OFFICERS

Judge: The symbol of the Judge is a Pair of Scales, and signifies "Equity." Each Assembly shall, at the annual election, elect a

Judge, who shall be a Judge throughout the Order; one Judge Advocate, and a Clerk of Court, who, together, shall constitute a Court for the trial of grievances, misdemeanours and breaches of law. The Judge shall patiently hear all charges which may require adjudication, and first effect a friendly settlement, if possible; if impossible, shall order an indictment and convene the Court, impartially hear all the evidence, and give the decision, which shall be binding; shall adjourn the Court from time to time, as the case may require, and sit in a sister Court when called to do so. The station is at the right and front of the Master Workman.

Judge Advocate: It shall be the duty of the Judge Advocate to prepare in writing all indictments, and issue all summonses when ordered by the Judge; to attend all sittings of the Court, and perform all of the duties of Prosecuting Attorney; and perform the like duties for a sister Court when called upon to do so. The station is at right of the Judge.

Clerk: It shall be the duty of the Clerk to attend all the sittings of the Court and keep a correct record of the proceedings; and serve all summonses, and perform all duties pertaining to the office; and perform like duties in a sister Court when called upon to do so. Station at the left of the Unknown Knight.

In case of sickness of, or if a charge be brought against an officer of any Court, the corresponding officer of a sister Assembly shall be called in form as follows:

The number of all the Local Assemblies of all the officers (of like grade) in the District, shall be placed in a wheel, to be drawn by such officer as the balance of the Court may direct; and the officer so drawn shall sit and discharge the duties.

Absence from the Court may be excused on account of sickness, or being at a distance of more than twenty (20) miles from the seat of Court, or such other unavoidable cause as the Court may deem sufficient. The prosecutor and accused may choose their counsel, who shall be members of the Order in good standing. In the case of the refusal or neglect of the accused to attend the Court, the charge shall be heard, a decision rendered, and the penalty fixed. Decisions shall be certified by the Court to the Assembly, and by it executed.

Appeals may be taken to the District Court, and from that to the General Assembly. In the case of Locals attached to the General Assembly, appeals may be had to the Court in Bane, composed of the Judges of the three nearest Locals, and from that to the General Assembly.

HISTORICAL SKETCH OF
THE KNIGHTS OF LABOR

(From March Number, 1886, Chicago "Knights of Labor")

The Order of the Knights of Labor was started in Philadelphia in 1869 by Uriah S. Stephens, a clothing cutter of that city, where many local assemblies were formed ere the movement spread to other localities. With Mr. Stephens were associated Frederick Turner and Joshua L. Wright. These three drew up the ritual and attended the birth of an absolutely secret society, and so well were the secrets of the order guarded that not even the name was divulged until 1881, and then only with the approval of the proper authorities.

THE HEAD OF THE ORDER of Knights of Labor is Terrance V. Powderly. He was born in Carbondale, Pa., January 24th, 1849. He learned the machinist's trade, and put in his spare time in educating himself in civil engineering. At the age of 19 he joined the Machinists' and Blacksmiths' Union of Scranton and became its presiding officer. Ten years ago he joined the Knights of Labor and became Secretary of District Assembly No. 16. He was active in bringing together the scattered threads

Therefore, we have formed the Order of Knights of Labor, for the purpose of organizing and directing the power of the industrial masses, not as a political party, for it is more – in it are crystallized sentiments and measures for the benefit of the whole people, but it should be borne in mind, when exercising the right of suffrage, that most of the objects herein set forth can only be obtained through legislation, and that it is the duty of all to assist in nominating and supporting with their votes only such candidates as will pledge their support to these measures, regardless of party. But no one shall, however, be compelled to vote with the majority, and calling upon all who believe in securing the "greatest good to the greatest number," to join and assist us, we declare to the world that our aims are:

1. To make industrial and moral worth, not wealth, the true standard of individual and National greatness.

2. To secure to the workers the full enjoyment of the wealth they create, sufficient leisure in which to develop their intellectual, moral and social faculties; all of the benefits, recreation and pleasures of association; in a word, to enable them to share in the gains and honors of advancing civilization.

In order to secure these results, we demand at the hands of the State:

3. The establishment of Bureaus of Labour Statistics that we may arrive at a correct knowledge of the educational, moral and financial condition of the labouring masses.

4. That the public lands, the heritage of the people, be reserved for actual settlers; not another acre for railroads or speculators; and that all lands now held for speculative purposes be taxed to

their full value.

5.   The abrogation of all laws that do not bear equally upon capital and labour, and the removal of unjust technicalities, delays and discriminations in the administration of justice.

6.   The adoption of measures providing for the health and safety of those engaged in mining, manufacturing and building industries, and for indemnification to those engaged therein for injuries received through lack of necessary safeguards.

7.   The recognition by incorporation of trades' unions, orders, and such other associations as may be organized by the working masses to improve their condition and protect their rights.

8.   The enactment of laws to compel corporations to pay their employees weekly, in lawful money, for the labour of the preceding week, and giving mechanics and labourers a first lien upon the product of their labour to the extent of their full wages.

9.   The abolition of the contract system on National, State and Municipal works.

10.   The enactment of laws providing for arbitration between employers and employed, and to enforce the decisions of the arbitrators.

11.   The prohibition, by law, of the employment of children under 15 years of age in workshops, mines and factories.

12.   To prohibit the hiring out of convict labour.

13.   That a graduated income tax be levied.

And we demand at the hands of Congress:

14.   The establishment of a National monetary system, in which a circulating medium in necessary quantity shall issue directly to the people, without the intervention of banks; that all the national issue shall be full legal tender in payment of all debts, public and private; and that the government shall not guarantee or recognize any private banks, or create any banking corporations.

15.   That interest-bearing bonds, bills of credit or notes shall never be issued by the Government, but that, when need arises, the emergency shall be met by issue of legal tender non-interest-bearing money.

16.   That the importation of foreign labour under contract be prohibited.

17.   That, in connection with the post-office, the Government shall organize financial exchanges, safe deposits, and facilities for deposit of the savings of the people in small sums.

18.   That the government shall obtain possession, by purchase, under the right of eminent domain, of all telegraphs, telephones and railroads, and that hereafter no charter or license be issued to any corporations for construction or operation of any means of transporting intelligence, passengers or freight.

And while making the foregoing demands upon the State and National Government, we will endeavour to associate our own labours:

19.   To establish co-operative institutions such as will tend to supersede the wage system, by the introduction of a co-operative industrial system.

20.   To secure for both sexes equal pay for equal work.

21.   To shorten the hours of labour by a general refusal to work for more than eight hours.

22.   To persuade employers to agree to arbitrate all differences which may arise between them and their employees, in order that the bonds of sympathy between them may be strengthened and that strikes may be rendered unnecessary.

COMMENTS

From the foregoing history we learn that Terrence V. Powderly joined the Knights of Labor in 1878. As he was so very prominent a labor agitator as to attain to the office of Mayor of Scranton, Pa., in 1877, the time of the greatest and most general labor troubles in this country; when great mobs, as professed champions of labor, appeared in most of our large cities and destroyed over $3,000,000 worth of rail road property in Pittsburgh, Pa., alone, and were only suppressed after much bloodshed; in Pittsburgh over 100 being killed, is there not reason to believe that Powderly was already at the head of the Knights of Labor? We are told that "so well were the secrets of the order guarded that not even the name was divulged until 1881, and then only with the approval of the proper authorities." Of course the proper authorities of the order would not wish to have it known that they were responsible for such loss of property and life. The fact that Mr. Powderly was then a Knight of Labor and so prominent as to be elected Mayor of a city like Scranton, and that while Mayor of that city "he was active in bringing together the scattered threads of the order, to form the first General Assembly in 1878," and yet did it all so secretly that the name of the order even was unknown to the public for three years more is very significant, and it requires no stretch of the imagination to believe that this secret order was the instigator of those labor mobs, which shook the nation in 1877 and did not dare reveal the existence of the order for the next four years.

Whether Governmental control of railroads, telegraphs and telephones would, as demanded by this order, be desirable, in view of the vast increase of political power and temptation to corruption that would inevitably follow is at least questionable. Nor does it seem wise, by abolishing the contract system, as to public improvements and purchases, to thereby prevent the competition, which bids and contracts afford, and thus vastly increase their cost. In No. 10 of their "declaration," compulsory arbitration between employers and employees is demanded. If the only question for arbitration was that of wages this would not be so objectionable, but the Knights of Labor claim a complete monopoly of labor. Not only do they demand of members of their order the most abject, unquestioning obedience, even when personally they have no grievance and to obey means great suffering, even for the necessaries of life, for themselves and families, but they say to employers, "ye shall neither hire or discharge a hand without our consent, for any reason, and we will fix the hours of labor and the wages that you shall pay." But the half has not yet been told: They say to every labourer, "join our gang or you shall have no work," and beginning with calling them names, such as "scab" and "rat," where freemen still refuse the lodge bondage, vilification, intimidation, the boycott, violence and murder are resorted to, towards such laborers, and any who may dare to employ them, as scores of strikes have proved, where the only grievance was the employment of a few men who refused to join the Knights of Labor. The McCormick strike and the two strikes of the Lake Shore railroad switchmen are fair examples of the demands of the order on this point.

The only grievance claimed by the order in either case was the employment of half a dozen non-union workmen of sober, industrious habits.

The notoriety given this secret order by the great Southwestern strike of the present year (1886) and the many strikes that followed it in all our large cities are fresh in the memory of all.

A man by the name of Hall, foreman of the Texas Pacific railroad shop at Marshall and a Knight of Labor is discharged, the company says for absence without leave, and he has never disproved the charge. Immediately a strike is ordered along the entire line of this road and as this did not have the desired effect a strike was ordered on the Missouri Pacific railroad also, and business in four States is paralysed for weeks, 30,000 railroad employees are in idleness and Satan finds mischief for them to do in trying to prevent others from taking their places, resulting in blood-shed, murder and destruction of property. For two months the fight is kept up; the loss to those directly concerned aggregating many millions of dollars and much more indirectly, by unsettling business all over the country. The companies succeed in operating their roads, in spite of the opposition, and when at last the Knights yield, it is to find their places very largely filled with men that the companies refuse to discharge.

Knights of Labor officials claim to have had other grievances besides the discharge of Hall. The following taken from "*Broadstreets Commercial Reports*" of March 13th, is quoted with approval in the "*Knights of Labor*" of March 1886.

"The Strike on the Texas Pacific and the Gould Southwestern railways naturally attracts most attention, crippling the traffic, as it does, of four states. The strike, so far as can be learned from Knights of Labor statements, is based on the refusal of the Texas Pacific to discharge seventy men, "as promised," who had been hired for a limited term, and instead of doing which the company discharged other and older workmen. The second point made is the unwarranted discharge of a Texas Pacific conductor, a Knight of Labor; and the third, the discharge of a foreman in the company's Marshall shops, an active Knight of Labor, without cause. The strike on the Texas Pacific not proving effective, the entire Missouri Pacific Knights of Labor were called out to strike to coerce the Texas Pacific. There are employed in this system about 30,000 men, and of these the Knights of Labor claim 9,000 members. They believe they can influence 4,000 more. The number of men actually reported on strike is about 6,000."

KNIGHTS OF LABOR AND ANARCHISM

In view of the violence and blood-shed attending the Southwestern and other strikes during 1886, and the fact that Parsons, and others not yet tried, who were engaged in the extensive murderous conspiracy which resulted in the Haymarket riot are known to be Knights of Labor, some have charged the order with the responsibility for the crime.

Whether the order, as such, was a party to that massacre or not may never be known. Had there been conclusive evidence that it was *directly* concerned in that crime it could never have withstood the wrath of a thoroughly aroused public and none knew this better than Mr. Powderly, who hastened to denounce Anarchism in unmeasured terms, and the Chicago "*Knights of Labor*" of May 8th printed the following on its first page entirely in capitals:

Let it be understood by all the world that the Knights of Labor have no affiliation, association, sympathy or respect for the band of cowardly murderers, cut-throats and robbers, known as anarchists, who sneak through the country like midnight assassins, stirring up the passions of ignorant foreigners, unfurling the red flag of anarchy and causing riot and blood-shed. Parsons, Spies, Fielding, Most and all their followers, sympathizers, aiders, and abettors should be summarily dealt with. They are entitled to no more consideration than wild beasts. The leaders are cowards and their followers are fools.

Knights of Labor boycott them; if one of the gang of scoundrels should by any mistake get access to our organization expel them at once, brand them as outlawed monsters. Do not even permit yourselves to hold conversation with one of them; treat them as they deserve to be treated, as human monstrosities not entitled to the sympathy or consideration of any person in the world.

We are sure we voice the sentiment of the entire organization when we say that we hope that Parsons, Spies, Most, Fielding and the whole gang of outlaws will be blotted from the face of the earth.

No one can complain that these denunciations are not strong enough. It is however interesting to observe how much more tenderly the anarchists are spoken of in later issues of the paper, and during their trial they are repeatedly referred to as "so-called anarchists." When the prominent Merchant Prince and Christian Philanthropist John V. Farwell, by request, furnished this paper a very sensible article on the labor question, Bert Stewart and another Knight of Labor champion, under the *nom de plume* of Wheelbarrow, attacked him with such vituperation as to call forth the following reply published in the issue of August 14th 1886.

Is Wheelbarrow a Workingman and a Christian?
To the Editor of the Knights of Labor

I am not in the habit of taking any notice of anonymous communications in criticizing my record or character, but "Wheelbarrow," in my opinion, has studied the four gospels, *wheelbarrow* fashion, instead of in a *locomotive* style, if he considers his letter a fair criticism of my article on the relations of labor to

arrests of late of men called anarchists and dynamiters, and our police judges have gotten off a wonderful mass of fustian about incendiary talk, and the need of suppressing it.

There is no such thing known to our system as an excess of free speech. It cannot be. The American sovereign is free to speak his mind on any subject connected with our public affairs.

There can be no limitation. He is free to say whatever he pleases in time of peace. He may declare the whole government a nest of traitors who should be hung, blown up, destroyed in a moment. He is free to denounce any public man in the same way. He is free to declare that it would be best to sweep all monopolists into the sea, and take their property for the public good. He is free to arm himself, and to advise all his fellows to do likewise, and be prepared to defend their rights against traitors and scoundrels who destroy our liberties."

In the issue of September 4th, is an article headed "*Knights of Labor Fable*," consisting of a dialogue between "*Casual Acquaintance*" and "*Man of Understanding*" in which "man of understanding" is made to advocate the doctrine that "not only the resources of nature but also the machinery that is used to aid the production and distribution of wealth should be worked by the people for their common good" including "mills, factories, railroads, telegraphs," etc. And he assures "Casual Acquaintance" that "the best minds of this generation are enlisted on the side of socialism."

In the same issue, on the editorial page, the Haymarket murderers whom we are told in the May 8th number are "deserving of no more consideration than wild beasts" and they hope will be "blotted from the surface of the earth" are referred to as martyrs and their expected execution as "judicial murder." We quote the following from the article which is signed "Diogenes."

"It will be stranger still after the judicial murders take place to those who think they have made political capital by their conviction to find the lightning of outraged justice has exploded their plans.

We are not in sympathy with anarchy, and this is well understood, and we are classified by them as a governmentalist, or a believer in the use of the ballot, and of liberty regulated by law.

But we have not read our history upside down, and everywhere it has taught us that a cause once baptized with blood moves forward with great rapidity. The blood of John Brown, though convicted and hung for the violation of the laws of Virginia, was the baptismal font of the abolition movement, the birth of the Republican Party.

May not the hanging of Parsons and his associates pass into future history the same? Those men will mount the scaffold as though it were the golden stairs to the gate of Heaven. They are no cowards, but zealots, of such stuff as martyrs are made of, and their followers will regard them as such and cherish their memory the same as the memory of John Brown is cherished by millions in this country today.

The murder of Joseph Smith by a drunken soldiery was the blood that baptized the Mormon Church and gave them a martyr. Well, at present writing it looks as though the anarchists are to have their martyrs, and the fools who have selected this method to crush out their ideas will find thousands springing up to crown them and keep their memories fresh and green.

Such is history, and when the names of judge, jury and attorneys have passed away and are forgotten, the memory of these men will live after them, not as painted now by the journals of today, but as heroes murdered in the name of law."

In the September 18th number is the following announcement on the first page: THE LIVES OF THE ANARCHISTS -

THE KNIGHTS OF LABOR will publish during the next three months the lives of the condemned anarchists, written by themselves. The sketches will be written exclusively for this paper, and will be accompanied by elegant engravings of original photographs. The KNIGHTS OF LABOR does this for the reason that we believe the American people are interested in giving every man a fair hearing; and it is but justice to these men to let them tell their own story in their own way.

The antipathy of the Knights of Labor to the Chinese is well, known, and unless repented of, should forfeit its members the sympathy of every citizen of the country.

In the March number of the "*Knights of Labor*" we find some significant facts on this point, in reference to the Seattle, Washington Territory riots, when 300 inoffensive Chinese were driven from their homes.

1. The first man of this mob, and doubtless its leader, who was arrested by Governor Squire was M. McMillan, Master Workman of the Knights of Labor.

2. Charles G. Stewart who was killed while resisting arrest was "a native-born American, and Odd-Fellow, a Knight Templar and member of the Grand Army of the Republic."

So vigorously have the Knights used the boycott that a single paragraph from the March "*Knights of Labor*" will suffice.

"The boycott, to be successful, must be vigorously pushed. Don't stop for friendship or anything else, for if the merchant with whom you trade is your friend he will never hesitate to assist you as much as possible in your fight for liberty. Don't buy one single article that is under boycott, no matter if your own brother keeps it. Don't get shaved in a barber shop unless it is a union shop. Don't smoke cigars unless they are union made cigars, and don't let the heathen Chinese do your washing. Don't forget these things. Stick to your principles and never forget to ask for union goods."

Mr. Powderly has had considerable to say in his so called secret circulars about boycotting the saloons, but we have heard of no assembly that has yet declared such a boycott and that the liquor party have no fears of such a boycott is evidenced by the following item taken from the "*Knights of Labor*" of September 4th:

"WILL RECOGNIZE THE KNIGHTS

PHILADELPHIA, August 31st – At a meeting of the Philadelphia Lager Beer Brewer's Association, held today, it was unanimously adopted that, beginning with this date, the association formally recognizes the Knights of Labor to the exclusion of all other labor organizations. Employers are requested to withdraw from the Workingmen's and Brewers' Unions and to associate themselves with the Knights of Labor. There will be no change in the hours of labor, wages or any other conditions acknowledged under the old union. The notice will be posted up in every brewery in Philadelphia tomorrow morning. How it will be received by the men remains to be seen. Trouble is expected, but the boss brewers are determined to stand by their action."

CONCLUSION

A sincere desire to aid Workingmen in their efforts to secure the greatest good to the greatest number; to make industrial and moral worth the true standard of greatness and to secure to workers the enjoyment of the wealth they create has led to the publication of this ritual of the Knights of Labor, together with an historical sketch of the order and its declaration of principles with quotations and comments.

This country is emphatically a workingman's country. Our moral, social and political opportunities are such as to make every citizen heir to an inheritance that millions of dollars could not buy. With an open bible before him, a common school in every neighborhood, a ballot in his hand and the government working by, with and for him, against caste and titled aristocracy; with a Father Almighty in heaven and a Savior calling by his Holy Spirit; every workingman, however humble, is a capitalist, in the largest and best sense of the word.

In pledging secrecy and obedience to the organization of the Knights of Labor for life, he signs away the right of private judgement, as it relates to many affairs, and becomes an abject vassal of a "committee," who use him as a tool to further the interests of a great monopoly, which loves "darkness rather than light, because its deeds are evil." A monopoly which compels its members to become the enemies of those which oppose it. The assassin, so far as possible, of the weal of workingmen who will not join it. With arrogance and oppression the order compels its members to resist the administration of law, when it conflicts with its supposed interests. It claims the right of monopolizing every industrial interest and while strengthening itself in this position at every possible point attempts to wage a war of extermination on all monopolies who question its right of supreme sway.

Such, as we understand it, is the nature of this young and dangerous monstrosity, which borrows from the graves of the dark ages the title ("Knight") long since made, in consequence of the progress of nations, a subject of just ridicule.

Since this order is sweeping in members from all parts of our beloved land and has already wrested from many toilers the opportunity of enjoying the wealth that they have created, by destroying it; having laid violent hands on their business and taken from them their wages; since it has caused them in some instances to be murdered and to become murderers; since it places them in a warlike attitude toward those persons and institutions which they should encourage and cherish, we publish this exposition. May it enlighten the minds of many brave and conscientious Knights of Labor (who have unwarily been lured by the bait and caught in the snare) to repent of their lack of circumspection, to confess and forsake this sin and warn their neighbors of the fraud.

It is also our desire to save the many, who have not yet been humbled and degraded by training in its ranks; the many who have not yet sold their birthright, in an hour when weary and oppressed by some scheming Jacob, for a mess of pottage, from joining the organization of the Knights of Labor.

Shall mystic bands with cruel hands,

Usurp and govern all the lands?

From sea to sea, from pole to pole

Shall men profess God's name in vain

In secret lodge for lust of Gain,

And sell the body with the soul?

Let light now shine with power divine,

To overthrow the base design

Of those who toil the young to gain;

Who strongly bind the noble mind,

In slavery's chains – until they find

They seek for liberty in vain.

Suggested Further Reading

Carnes, Mark C. *Secret Ritual and Manhood in Victorian America* New Haven: Yale University Press 1989

Cook, Ramsay *The Regenerators: Social Criticism in Late Victorian English Canada* Toronto: University of Toronto Press 1985

Fones-Wolf, Kenneth *Trade Union Gospel: Christianity and Labor in Industrial Philadelphia1865-1915* Philadelphia: Temple University Press 1989

Homel, Gene Howard *Fading Beams of the Nineteenth Century: Radicalism and Early Socialism in Canada's 1890s* *Labour/Le Travail* 5 (Spring 1980) 7-32

James, Dr. Bob *Secret Societies and the Labour Movement* Tighes Hill, Australia: self-published catalogue to an exhibit at the 6th Biennial Conference of the Australian Society for the study of Labour History 1999

Kealey, Gregory and Palmer, Bryan *Dreaming of What Might Be* New Hogtown Press 1987

Marks, Lynne *Revivals and Roller Rinks* Toronto: University of Toronto Press 1996

Marks, Lynne *The Knights of Labor and the Salvation Army: Religion and Working-Class Culture in Ontario, 1882-1890* *Labour/Le Travail* 28 (Fall 1991) 89-127

Phelan, Craig *Grand Master Workman – Terence Powderly and the Knights of Labor* Westport CT: Greenwood Press 2000

Powderly, Terence Vincent *The Path I Trod: the autobiography of Terence V. Powderly* ed. Harry J. Carman, Henry David, and Paul N. Guthrie. New York: AMS Press 1968

Thompson, Phillips *The Politics of Labor* (1887) reprinted with an introduction by Jay Atherton, Toronto: University of Toronto Press 1975

Verzuh, Ron *Radical Rag: The Pioneer Labour Press in Canada* Ottawa: Steel Rail Press 1988

Weir, Robert E. *Beyond Labor's Veil: the culture of the Knights of Labor* University Park PA: Pennsylvania St